W9-BKX-394

Inventors

Carlotta Hacker

Weigl

CALGARY
www.weigl.com

This series is dedicated to all Canadians who take pride in their communities and their citizenship; and to those who will continue to help build a strong Canada. The Canadians in this series have helped to build Canada by being outstanding in their fields, from literature to business, sports to the arts. Some have overcome great obstacles to make their dreams come true, and their dedication and achievement serve as an inspiration for young and old alike.

Published by Weigl Educational Publishers Limited
6325 – 10 Street SE
Calgary, Alberta, Canada
T2H 2Z9
Website: http://www.weigl.com
Copyright © 2000 WEIGL EDUCATIONAL PUBLISHERS LIMITED

Canadian Cataloguing in Publication Data

Hacker, Carlotta, 1931–
    Great Canadian inventors

    (Great Canadians)
    Includes bibliographical references and index.
    ISBN 1-896990-47-9

    1. Inventors—Canada—Biography—Juvenile literature. 2. Inventions—Canada—History—Juvenile literature. I. Title. II. Series: Great Canadians (Calgary, Alta.)
T39.H32 2000   j609.2'271   C00-910051-2

Printed in Canada
1 2 3 4 5 6 7 8 9 0   04 03 02 01 00

Editor
Rennay Craats
Design
Warren Clark
Cover Design
Terry Paulhus
Copy Editor
Megan Lappi
Layout
Katherine Phillips

Photograph Credits
Every reasonable effort has been made to trace ownership and to obtain permission to reprint copyright material. The publishers would be pleased to have any errors or omissions brought to their attention so that they may be corrected in subsequent printings

Academy of Motion Picture Arts and Sciences: page 42; Courtesy of Wilfred Bigelow: pages 12, 13, 14, 15, 16, 17; Glenbow Archives, Calgary, Canada: pages 8, 9; Imax Corporation: page 43; Estate of Gertrude Le Caine: pages 25, 26, 27; Dr. Julia Levy: pages 30, 31, 32, 33, 34, 35; Audrey McQuarrie: page 44; Musee J. Armand Bombardier: pages 18, 19, 20, 21, 22, 23; Naismith Museum & Hall of Fame, Almonte, Ontario: pages 37, 41; National Archives of Canada: pages 6, 7, 10, 11, 36, 38, 39, 40; National Research Council of Canada: pages 24, 28; Courtesy of Paul Pedersen: page 29; Rachel Zimmerman: page 45.

CONTENTS

6
Alexander Graham Bell

12
Wilfred Bigelow

18
Joseph-Armand Bombardier

24
Hugh Le Caine

30
Julia Levy

36
James Naismith

MORE GREAT CANADIANS

Nestor Burtnyk	42
Tim Collings	42
Georges-Edouard Desbarats	42
Graeme Ferguson	43
Reginald Fessenden	43
Sir Sandford Fleming	43
James Hillier	44
Harold Johns	44
Audrey McQuarrie	44
Bruce Nodwell	45
Sir Charles Saunders	45
Rachel Zimmerman	45
Glossary	46
Suggested Reading	47
Index	48

Inventors

Canadians have played an important part in science, entertainment, music, medicine, and sports through their inventions. If it were not for Canadian inventors, people might never have played basketball, listened to electronic music, or raced across the snow on a snowmobile. But there are many other Canadians who have made exciting discoveries. Hundreds of Canadians have invented things, ranging from small gadgets to important ways of treating disease.

Here are a few of the many things that have been invented by Canadians: four sports—basketball, hockey, lacrosse, and Canadian football; the CANDU reactor that uses nuclear energy to create electricity; Pablum baby food; an anti-gravity flying suit; Easy-Off oven cleaner; radio broadcasting; the toboggan; insulin to treat people with diabetes; the slicklicker to clean up oil spills; the board game Trivial Pursuit; the telephone; frozen food; IMAX movies; and the paint roller.

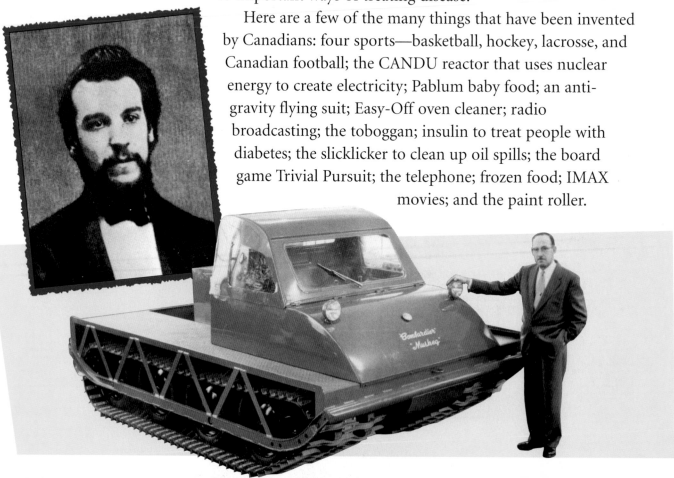

After people invent something, they often want to **patent** it so that nobody else can make or sell it without their permission. The Canadian Innovation Centre in Waterloo, Ontario, advises people on how to do this. A search of the Internet can also lead to other groups connected with Canadian inventors. Right across the country, there are many people who are full of clever ideas about how to do or make something.

The Suggested Reading list at the end of this book will help you find out about these inventions and many others. It may also encourage you to get creative and become an inventor.

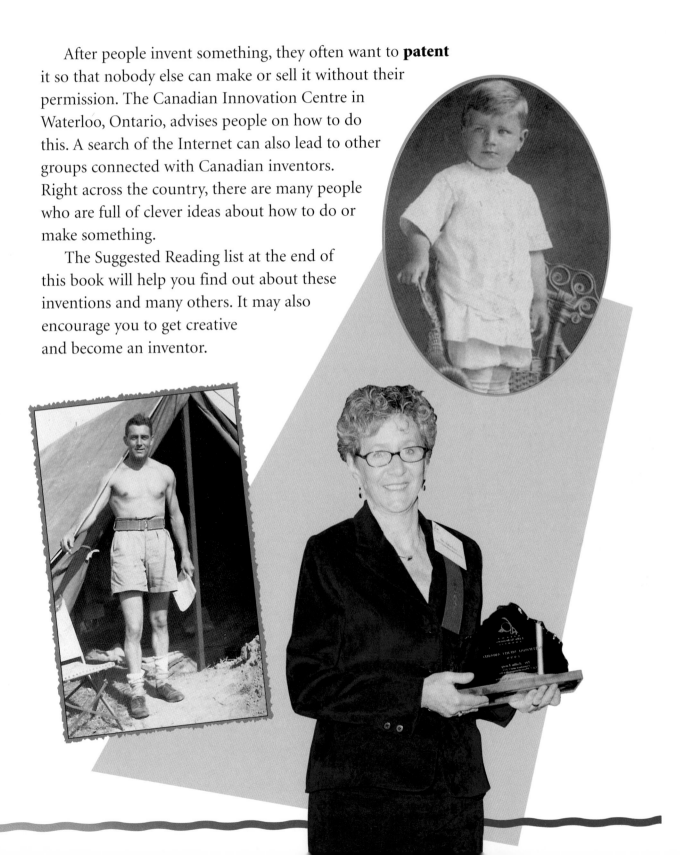

Alexander Graham Bell

1847-1922

> ❝ If I could make a current of electricity vary in intensity precisely as air varies in density during the production of sound, I would be able to transmit speech electrically. ❞

Key Events

1870 Moves with parents to Canada

1871 Begins teaching at Boston School for Deaf Mutes

1873 Is appointed professor of vocal physiology at Boston University

1874 Has idea for inventing the telephone

1876 Speaks first words ever heard through telephone and makes the world's first long-distance call

1877 Marries Mabel Hubbard

1890 Founds American Association for the Promotion of Teaching of Speech to the Deaf

1907 Forms Aerial Experiment Association

1919 Sets water speed record with hydrofoil

Early Years

Aleck Bell stared at the sign his father had drawn on the blackboard. Then he turned around, faced the audience, and growled like an angry dog.

The people in the audience were not shocked. Instead, they clapped. They were being given a demonstration of a system called Visible Speech, which Aleck's father had invented. Visible Speech was a type of alphabet, a way of writing down different sounds. It helped teach speech to people who could neither hear nor speak. Aleck was helping to show how it worked.

Aleck and his family lived in Edinburgh, Scotland, where his father taught **elocution**. By the time Aleck was in his teens, he knew a lot about how sounds were made. He and his two brothers once made a "speaking machine" that produced human sounds. They surprised their neighbours by getting the machine to cry, "Mama! Mama!"

> " *Every moment of my time is devoted to the study of electricity and experiments.* "

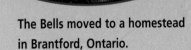

The Bells moved to a homestead in Brantford, Ontario.

Backgrounder

Helping People to Speak

If you are born without hearing, you do not know what words sound like, so speech does not come naturally. Alexander Melville Bell, Aleck's father, made up a symbol for each sound made by a person's tongue, lips, teeth, and vocal cords. With practice, even people who lacked hearing could learn to make the right noise for each symbol.

During his demonstrations of Visible Speech, Melville sent his sons out of the room. He then asked people in the audience to make a noise—any noise. Melville wrote the symbols for those noises on the blackboard. His sons were called back into the room and read the symbols and produced the appropriate noises or words. These demonstrations helped spread news of Visible Speech so that the system could be used to help people learn to speak.

Developing Skills

Aleck attended the Royal High School in Edinburgh and then took university courses in Edinburgh and London. But much of his education was gained from members of his own family. His mother taught him the piano. His father taught him the mechanics of sound. His grandfather gave him the run of his library.

Aleck spent a year with his grandfather in London, eagerly reading books that had information on sound—books on acoustics, the tuning of instruments, the human ear. He was particularly interested in how the ear worked, because his mother had difficulty hearing. But it was not his mother's health that was worrying the family at this time. It was the health of Aleck's brothers. Both of them were sick with **tuberculosis**.

By 1870, both brothers had died of the disease. Fearing that Aleck might die, too, his father decided to move the family to Canada. He thought of Canada as a healthy place. The family settled in Brantford, Ontario, alongside the Grand River. As it turned out, Aleck spent only the holidays there. His father found him a job in Boston, Massachusetts, teaching Visible Speech in a school for children who could not hear.

Aleck arrived in Boston in 1871 and soon became well known for his teaching methods. In 1873, he was appointed a professor of voice **physiology** at Boston University. Meanwhile, he stayed up night after night doing experiments. He was trying to find a way of sending several electric messages down a single telegraph wire at the same time.

Aleck was hired as a professor at Boston University because of his abilities rather than formal education.

When Aleck was home for the holidays in the summer of 1874, he continued to puzzle over this problem. While he was doing so, another thought came to him. He realized that it might be possible to send the sound of a human voice along a wire. This was a very exciting idea. It meant that people far apart would actually be able to speak to each other.

Back in Boston in 1875, Aleck hired Thomas Watson to help him with the project. Thomas was an electrical worker who knew more about electricity than Aleck did. They made an excellent team.

Aleck and Thomas Watson (below) became fast friends during their experiments.

" *I think that transmission of the human voice is much nearer than I had supposed.* "

Backgrounder

The Telegraph

The telegraph was invented by Samuel Morse, who demonstrated it to the United States Congress in 1844. Messages were sent along telegraph wires using the Morse code, long and short bursts of electric current. For instance, one short burst (a dot) followed by one long burst (a dash) is the code for the letter "a."

The telegraph was a great breakthrough. It meant that people far apart could communicate directly. By the 1860s, most large towns were connected by telegraph lines. In 1866, there was another great advance when an underwater cable was laid across the Atlantic Ocean between Newfoundland and Ireland. News of events in Europe could now reach North America immediately. Even so, everything had to be spelled out letter by letter using dots and dashes.

Accomplishments

> *All really big discoveries are the result of thought.*

hroughout 1875, Aleck and Thomas worked on their project. They set up a laboratory in the attic of a Boston house. In one room, they placed the **transmitter** that Thomas made. In the other room, they put the receiver. By the end of the year, they were able to send "voice sounds" along the wire connecting the transmitter and receiver, but the words were not clear.

On March 10, 1876, the two inventors were ready to try out an improved model of the transmitter. Aleck was sitting beside it when he accidentally spilled acid on his pants. "Mr. Watson— come here! I want to see you!" he shouted. Thomas, who was in the other room, heard the words through the receiver.

The two men were so excited that they danced a jig. To mark the importance of this first telephone message, they spoke into the transmitter, saying "God Save the Queen." Later that year, they made the world's first long-distance telephone call. It was between Brantford and Paris, Ontario.

The invention of the telephone made Aleck very wealthy. He was able to sponsor other inventions. In 1907, he formed the Aerial Experiment Association for a group who wanted to build flying machines. By this time, Aleck was living permanently in the United States, but he had a vacation home at Baddeck, Nova Scotia.

Thomas Watson's and Aleck's experiments during the summer of 1875 led to the first telephone patent in the spring of 1876.

Backgrounder

Aleck's Other Inventions

Aleck and the young Canadian inventor, Casey Baldwin, experimented with machines that could skim across the surface of the water. The **hydrofoil** they launched in 1919 shot across Baddeck Bay at 110 kilometres per hour—faster than anything had ever travelled on water. Aleck also experimented with turning sea water into fresh water so that shipwrecked sailors would not die of thirst. He developed a way of making phonographic records on wax discs. Aleck invented the audiometer, a device for testing hearing. Displays of his inventions are shown at the Alexander Graham Bell Museum at Baddeck, Nova Scotia.

Aleck built this tetrahedral kite in his laboratory at Beinn Bhreagh. Although he patented and publicized this invention, it never caught on.

▶▶▶▶▶▶

QUICK NOTES

▶ Aleck chose his middle name, Graham. His parents had given him only one name, Alexander, after his father and grandfather.

▶ Aleck married Mabel Hubbard, one of his first students in Boston. She had lost her hearing as a young child, when she was seriously ill with scarlet fever.

▶ Aleck's summer home at Baddeck was called Beinn Bhreagh. This means "beautiful mountain" in Gaelic, a Scottish language.

The Baddeck property was huge, with plenty of space for trying out flying machines. Aleck made some strange-looking kites that were big enough to carry a person. The first kite to do so was the *Cygnet* in 1907. Aleck and his team also designed some of the earliest gasoline-powered airplanes. In 1909, he watched Douglas McCurdy fly the *Silver Dart* over the Bras d'Or Lakes near Baddeck. The *Silver Dart* was the first plane ever to fly in Canada.

While continuing with such experiments, Aleck remained true to his first interest—helping people who could not hear well. He donated large sums of money to set up schools and training programs for children with hearing problems. He gave speeches on the subject and helped in every way he could. Even after he was known worldwide as a famous inventor, Aleck continued to list his profession as "teacher of the deaf."

1913–

Wilfred Bigelow

> " It was one of the very few basic medical discoveries where no one stood up to say they'd done something similar. "

Key Events

1938 Graduates M.D. and M.S., University of Toronto

1941 Marries Ruth Burns-Jennings

1941–45 Serves overseas in Royal Canadian Army Medical Corps

1946 Appointed research fellow at Johns Hopkins Hospital in Baltimore, Maryland

1947 Begins research on hypothermia and becomes head of Heart Surgery at Toronto General Hospital

1949–50 Develops the heart pacemaker

1952 Improves hypothermia technique so that it is safe enough for use on humans

1958 Organizes Canada's first university training program for heart surgeons

1970–72 Serves as President at the Canadian Cardiovascular Society

1981 Is made an Officer of the Order of Canada

1992 Is awarded the Starr Medal of the Canadian Medical Association

1996 Is elected to the Canadian Medical Hall of Fame

Early Years

Nobody ever had to wonder what Bill Bigelow would be when he grew up. He wanted to be a surgeon like his father. Bill's father had been both doctor and surgeon to patients in the small towns of Manitoba, visiting them by horse and buggy. He had formed Canada's first private medical clinic in Brandon, Manitoba.

Bill spent his childhood in Brandon and later attended Brentwood College in Victoria, British Columbia. He completed his education at the University of Toronto, graduating in 1938 as doctor of medicine and master of surgery.

Three years later, while working as a resident surgeon at Toronto General Hospital, Bill operated on a young man with frostbitten fingers. The fingers had developed **gangrene** and had to be cut off. After the operation, Bill began to wonder why frostbite led to gangrene. He became very curious about the effects of extreme cold. This curiosity was to have far-reaching effects.

Wilfred (left) with sisters Agnes and Mary spent their early years in Brandon, Manitoba.

Backgrounder

Family Influence

Bill's parents, Grace and Wilfred, encouraged their children to do their best at whatever they tackled. But they did not let them get swollen-headed about their achievements. When Bill and his brother Dan were at medical school, they thought they knew a lot, but their father stressed how much they still had to learn. He wanted them always to have open minds so that they would remain curious and not take things for granted. He thought that it was important to think for oneself and not be overawed by what older and more senior people say.

Developing Skills

As a World War II front line surgeon, Bill slept in a trench covered by a canvas tent.

World War II was underway by the time Bill completed his training. He served in the Royal Canadian Army Medical Corps, landing on the Normandy beaches in France and operating on wounded soldiers on the battlefield. Some of the soldiers had such deep cuts in an arm or leg that the blood could not circulate in that limb.

Bill's research led him to believe that if he kept a wounded limb very cold, it would use less oxygen. As a result, it would not suffer much harm when the blood stopped circulating. He persuaded the British War Office to build him a special cooling cabinet for soldiers with badly wounded limbs. His aim was to protect the limbs from lack of oxygen so that they would not have to be **amputated**.

After the war, Bill spent a year at Johns Hopkins Hospital in Baltimore, Maryland, where he gained further experience. The surgeons in Baltimore were trying to find a way of operating on the heart—as were many other surgeons. In Philadelphia, for instance, John Gibbon was developing a machine that he hoped would take over the heart's pumping action while an operation was being performed.

Bill had different ideas. He thought that if cooling protected a limb, it might also protect the whole body. If a patient's body was made very cold, it might suffer no harm from lack of oxygen when the heart was stopped for a short while. This cooling process is called **hypothermia**.

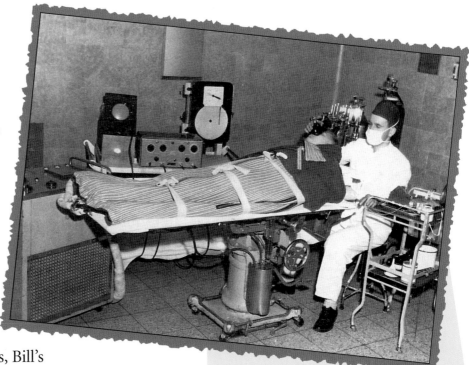

The refrigerator on the left cools the patient's body temperature for open-heart surgery.

In Toronto in 1947, Bill was put in charge of a team of researchers to carry out experiments on hypothermia. The leading members of this team included Bill's colleague John Callaghan and John Hopps, who was based at the National Research Council in Ottawa.

Like other researchers, Bill's team did their work on animals. First, a dog was given an **anesthetic** so that it did not feel anything. Then it was wrapped in cooling blankets and ice packs to lower its temperature. Since the room was kept freezing cold, the researchers also were very chilly, despite their thick clothing.

Nevertheless, their research went well. By 1950, they had proved that, with hypothermia, an animal's heart could be stopped for ten minutes or more without causing damage. Now they had to find a way of making the procedure safe enough to use on humans.

Backgrounder

The Beating Heart

For many years, surgeons could not do major heart operations because they could not allow the heart to stop beating. The heart is the pump that propels blood around the body through the blood vessels. As the blood circulates, it supplies the body with oxygen. If any part of the body is without oxygen for as little as five minutes, it can be seriously harmed. This presented surgeons with a big problem. Only if the heart lay still could they operate. Likewise, only if the blood was stopped from flowing through the heart could surgeons see what they were doing. Yet if they stopped the heart or stopped the blood from circulating, the patient would die.

Accomplishments

In 1950, Bill reported the results of his research at a meeting of surgeons in Colorado. His report caused great excitement. All over the world, research surgeons began to experiment with hypothermia.

By 1952, the Toronto surgeons were ready to perform the world's first open-heart operation using hypothermia. They began searching for a suitable patient. To their surprise, a surgeon in Minneapolis used the Toronto cooling technique on a human. Despite Bill's disappointment at not being the first, he was pleased that his theory had proved to be correct.

Soon hospitals in Toronto and other cities were doing open-heart surgery regularly. At first, they used hypothermia for the operation. Later, many used the heart-lung pump developed by John Gibbon in Philadelphia. This machine was first used on a human in 1953. It was connected by tubes to the patient's body so that, during an operation, blood was channelled through the pump, by-passing the heart. Surgeons using the heart lung-pump also used hypothermia because it made the operation safer.

Bill (left), John Callaghan, and John Hopps hold the first pacemaker.

Backgrounder

The Heart Pacemaker

Bill and his team invented the heart pacemaker. Work on this device started almost by accident. One day, during a hypothermia operation on a dog, the animal's heart stopped beating. Bill poked the heart with a metal **probe** he was holding. To his surprise, the heart started beating again, and the dog recovered completely. This set the researchers on a new line of thought. They found that they could use electricity to start a stopped heart and then keep it beating regularly. In 1950, John Hopps built a machine that would do this. The first heart pacemaker in the world was too large to put inside a person's chest. However, about ten years later, after transistor batteries became available, small enough pacemakers could be made.

Bill had started the "First Ice Age" in surgery. Meanwhile, he and his team continued their research on hypothermia. Much of their work was done on groundhogs, because these animals have something inside the body that lowers their temperature each winter when they hibernate. Bill's team never did manage to find out what the cooling agent was, but their research led to a greater understanding of hypothermia.

Because of Bill's work, longer and much more complicated operations have become possible. Hypothermia opened the door to great advances in surgery on the brain as well as the heart. Bill has made a major contribution in another way, too. In 1958, he set up a special program to train heart surgeons in Toronto. For many years, he was professor of surgery at the University of Toronto and also head of surgery at Toronto General Hospital.

Over the years, Bill has received many honours, yet he is very humble about his achievements. "I was in the right place at the right time," he says. "The real secret, of course, is to have the right people working with you."

▷▷▷▷▷▷

QUICK NOTES

▷ During their research on hypothermia, Bill and his team were the first people in the world ever to see inside a living heart while it was beating.
▷ Bill's book *Cold Hearts* (1984) describes the research on hypothermia.
▷ Bill's family has lived in Canada since 1761, when Isaac Bigelow moved to Nova Scotia from New England.

" *We've started a new Ice Age.* "

Bill enjoys a happy retirement with his wife, Ruth.

1907–1964

Joseph-Armand Bombardier

> **"** To succeed in life, one needs strength of character to do without self-indulgence and never to back down in the face of whatever obstacles stand in the way. **"**

Key Events

1922 Makes first snowmobile

1926 Starts his own business with the Garage Bombardier

1929 Marries Yvonne Labrecque

1937 Obtains patent for B7 snowmobile

1943 Designs an armoured snowmobile for the military

1953 Begins production of a muskeg tractor

1959 Starts selling the Ski-Doo

Early Years

On New Year's Eve 1922, the quiet of Valcourt, Quebec, was shattered by the roaring of an engine. The noise was so loud that it scared the horses. People ran from their houses to see what was happening.

They could not believe their eyes. Fifteen-year-old Armand Bombardier and his brother Léopold were driving over the snow on a strange vehicle. It had a wooden propeller at the back, attached to a rusty old engine. The whole thing was balanced on four runners, which had been part of an old sleigh.

Armand drove this homemade snowmobile for a kilometre, pretending he could not hear his father shouting at him to stop. His father was furious. He had given Armand the engine to practice on, but he had not expected the boy to make this dangerous machine. That night, he made Armand take the snowmobile apart.

To power his first snowmobile, Armand used a propeller and the engine from an old Ford Model T.

Backgrounder

The Young Inventor

From an early age, Armand was intrigued by anything mechanical. He spent long hours in a shed on his father's farm, making machines out of old bits of equipment. He made a toy tractor that moved on its own. He made a small cannon that fired. By the time Armand was thirteen, he knew how to fix broken engines. His neighbours often called on him for help. Even so, they were surprised when he made a machine that could propel itself across the snow.

Developing Skills

Although Armand's first snowmobile had moved across the snow, it was an experiment rather than a usable machine. All sorts of improvements were needed. In the first place, the whirling propeller was very dangerous, and it could only propel the machine forward. The vehicle could not go in reverse.

Armand knew that he still had a lot to learn about mechanics and electrical engineering. When he was seventeen, he worked for a few months in a local auto-repair shop and then went to Montreal to gain more experience. There, he worked in a garage during the daytime. In the evenings, he took a course to upgrade his skills.

> ❝ The only way to convince people that it is possible to travel over snow is to do it. ❞

After two years, Armand was ready to start his own business. With his father's help, he bought a plot of land in Valcourt and opened the Garage Bombardier. Before long, his brother Léopold and other family members joined him.

The garage did well from the start, largely because of Armand's cleverness with machines. The government had not yet brought hydro lines to Valcourt, so none of the houses had electricity. Armand soon changed that. He built a dam and **turbine** on a stream near his garage to provide it with electric power.

Armand (middle back) was the oldest son in a large French-Canadian family.

In 1929, Armand married and began raising a family. Meanwhile, he continued to puzzle about how to build a better snowmobile. His neighbours in Valcourt became used to seeing him moving across the snow in odd machines. Armand still did not have a workable model in 1934—the winter that his son Yvon had an attack of appendicitis. Since there was no quick way of getting the boy to hospital, Yvon died.

The factory that manufactured the B7 could barely keep up with demand for the popular snowmobile.

This tragedy spurred Armand on to complete a snow machine. By 1936, he was making such headway that he applied to Ottawa for a patent. The patent would prevent other mechanics from copying his idea and making a similar machine. Armand called this snowmobile the B7, because it could carry seven people.

Backgrounder

Why Were Snowmobiles Needed?

In the early 1900s, winter travel was very difficult in Canada. There were no snowploughs to clear the roads. City streets were shovelled clear, but most roads in the countryside were buried under snow. Consequently, cars could not be driven in small towns and villages. If people wanted to visit another village, they went by horse-drawn sleigh, or they walked there on snowshoes. Both these forms of transport were slow. If a farmer had an accident, he could not be rushed to hospital. There was a great need for some form of quick and easy transport.

Accomplishments

At the beginning of 1937, Armand changed the name of his garage to L'Auto-Neige Bombardier (auto-neige is the French word for "snowmobile"). He had decided to stop doing automobile repairs so that he could concentrate on building snowmobiles. In June, he at last heard from Ottawa that his patent had been granted. This was great news. Armand now had a legal document saying that the invention belonged to him alone.

Armand had already sold several snowmobiles, and he quickly made twenty-five more. Most of them were bought by country doctors. Taxi and bus services were also eager to buy the vehicles. In 1938, a B7 cost $1,400. Armand advertised the machine by driving it across country after heavy snowstorms. On these trips, he went as far from home as Quebec City and Montreal. Orders poured in, and a hundred machines were in the works when World War II broke out in 1939.

The war had an immediate effect on Armand's business. He could not get the engines he needed. The government wanted military vehicles, which made it hard for companies to produce anything else. Armand moved with the times and began to design armoured snowmobiles and other similar military vehicles.

Armand and his company helped with the war effort by designing and building military vehicles during World War II.

In the 1950s, production shifted to vehicles like the Muskeg Tractor that could be used in the mining, oil, and forestry industries.

After the war, the Bombardier company did wonderfully well at first. Armand built various types of snowmobile, which became very popular. But in the late 1940s, sales suddenly dropped off. The Quebec government had begun a program of snow clearing. All major roads were cleared of snow so that cars could travel along them in winter.

Armand quickly adapted to this situation. He started making vehicles that could be used in rough country. Mining and forestry companies needed tractors that could travel across marshy ground without sinking in, and they were eager to buy Armand's machines.

Most of Armand's vehicles were designed to carry a number of passengers, but he now set to work on a snowmobile for just one or two riders. In 1959, he produced the Ski-Doo. Armand made the Ski-Doo for trappers and other people travelling in the North. But he realized it would be fun to ride, so he advertised it as a sport vehicle. The Ski-Doo was an immediate hit, and it became the most popular of all Armand's inventions. It is still popular today.

> " *The purpose of my invention is to make more practical the operation of a winter automobile in any road conditions.* "

Backgrounder

The Bombardier Company

Armand died just when the Ski-Doo was becoming popular, so he did not live to see the great snowmobile boom of the late 1960s and early 1970s. Armand's family carried on the business, branching out into other areas. Since Armand's death, the Bombardier company has made trains, airplanes, and a range of other products, which have been sold in many parts of the world. One of the most popular Bombardier products is the Sea-Doo, a type of Ski-Doo that travels across water.

1914–1977

Hugh Le Caine

> 66 **My primary concern was making an electronic instrument that was musically expressive.** 99

Key Events

1937 Makes his first electronic organ

1939 Gains M.Sc. degree in physical engineering from Queen's University, Kingston

1940 Joins National Research Council of Canada

1945–48 Makes Electronic Sackbut

1948 Goes to Birmingham University, England, to study nuclear physics

1952 Gains Ph.D. degree from Birmingham University

1954 Opens a music laboratory at the National Research Council

1955 Composes *Dripsody*

1957 Completes Touch-Sensitive Organ

1960 Marries Trudi Janowski

1964 Completes Multi-Track Tape Recorder

1970 Completes the Polyphone

Early Years

Hugh made his first musical instrument when he was four years old. It was only a board with some nails in it. But Hugh noticed that when he hit the nails with another nail, they seemed to go "ping!"

Hugh lived in Port Arthur, Ontario, which is now part of Thunder Bay. His father was an electrical engineer and his mother was a teacher. Both parents encouraged Hugh to use his imagination—and Hugh did. He made up games for his friends to play. He made up a secret language, which only he and his sister knew. He even tried to make an electronic guitar.

Electricity fascinated Hugh. He used it in all sorts of ways. He was especially proud of the secret bell he had put in his bedroom. It rang when his mother came upstairs to check if he had gone to bed. As soon as Hugh heard the bell, he snapped off the light and pretended to be asleep.

> " I tend to see scientists as children, who ... prefer to spend their time on games of their own invention. "

Hugh survived a deadly flu epidemic when he was just four years old.

Backgrounder

A Musical Beginning

Hugh's mother taught him the piano, and he began to play in public when he was six. Hugh had "perfect pitch." For instance, if he was asked to sing the note called Middle C, he could sing it exactly without hearing it on an instrument. Because of this, Hugh was very interested in pitch and in the sounds made by different musical instruments. There were several instruments in his home, including a piano, violin, and guitar. He checked out each one to see how it worked and how it made the different sounds.

Developing Skills

After Hugh graduated from high school, he enrolled in the Applied Science Program at Queen's University in Kingston, Ontario. He hoped to train as an electrical engineer, but he kept his interest in music. During summer vacation, Hugh studied piano in Toronto at the Conservatory of Music. He practised eight hours every day.

Hugh not only played music, but he listened to it at concerts, always analysing how particular sounds were made. He was especially interested in the new electronic instruments. A church in Kingston was the first place in Canada to have an electronic organ made by the American inventor, Laurens Hammond. Hugh was allowed to play it. He also tried out the Canadian-made Robb organ. In 1937, while Hugh was still a student at Queen's, he made his own electronic organ.

After gaining his bachelor's and master's degrees, Hugh moved on to the National Research Council (NRC) in Ottawa in 1940. By this time, World War II had started, so the NRC was concentrating on military work. Hugh did research on **radar** systems to locate enemy planes and ships. He also helped fellow workers with their projects. He had quickly gained a reputation for being an "ideas man," so researchers went to him for suggestions when they ran into problems in their work.

In 1938, Hugh worked in the Queen's University physics laboratory as a graduate student.

As well as being known as a problem solver, Hugh was known for his odd working hours. He thought that in an eight-hour work day, people are at their peak only for the first four hours. After that, they get tired and do not work well. So Hugh fitted two twelve-hour "days" into each twenty-four hour period. He worked for four hours, relaxed for four hours, and slept for four hours. Then he began the next "day" with another four hours' work.

When the war ended in 1945, Hugh no longer had to do military research. He could now research electronic music. But the NRC did not want to start a big research project on the subject. What was Hugh to do? He did not want to leave the NRC.

Hugh loved riding his motorcycles. He rode one for most of his adult life.

Backgrounder

Electronic Music

In electronic music, the sounds are made or changed electronically. The first people to make electronic music used door buzzers and other devices.

In the 1920s, Frank Morse Robb of Belleville, Ontario, made an organ that sounded like a church organ but was smaller. It did not use huge pipes to make the sound. Instead, it used shaped discs, which produced electric currents when turned at various speeds. Robb's was the first electronic organ ever to be made and sold, but it was not as popular as the American-made Hammond organ.

In the 1940s and 1950s, as scientists learned more about physics and nuclear physics, more ways were found of making electronic music. Today, there is an even greater variety.

> ❝ Every sound was exciting.... To be able to isolate a single sound and play it even twice was an experience, and you could hear it as long as you wanted to.... I remember making five hundred splices in one weekend. ❞

Accomplishments

Hugh decided to stay on at the NRC doing scientific work, and to do research on electronic music in his spare time. He told friends that he wanted to design electronic instruments that made a "beautiful sound." The Hammond and Robb organs sounded too mechanical, he said. He thought they were uninteresting. Hugh's aim was to make electronic music that was really musical.

In Ottawa, Hugh rented a house, which he turned into a workshop. Here, Hugh built his first successful electronic instrument. He called it the Electronic Sackbut. The sackbut is a medieval wind instrument—a type of early trombone. However, Hugh's instrument did not look at all like a trombone.

Hugh's Electronic Sackbut stood on its own stand, with a sheet of plywood covering the electronic parts. At the front was a piano-type keyboard, on which one note could be played at a time. Each note sounded louder or softer depending on how hard Hugh pressed it. When he slid his finger to the right or left, the sound slid too, getting higher or lower depending on which way Hugh slid his finger. Each note could make a variety of musical sounds.

Hugh demonstrated the electronic sackbut through the 1950s.

Completed in 1948, the Electronic Sackbut is now regarded as the first **synthesizer**. It attracted a lot of attention, and in 1954, the NRC at last let Hugh work full time on electronic music. Three years later, he completed an electronic organ that was "touch-sensitive" like the Sackbut. Meanwhile, he was also designing a tape recorder with several tracks. He went on to design many other instruments.

Hugh also composed music. His best-known piece is called *Dripsody*. It is made entirely from the sound of a drop of water falling into a bucket. After recording the sound, Hugh recorded it again and again at different speeds. His compositions were made to show the great variety of things that could be done with electronic music.

As well, Hugh helped set up electronic music studios at the University of Toronto and other universities. He designed equipment that helped inventive musicians compose original music. In many ways, he influenced the music that is heard today.

In 1974, at the age of sixty, Hugh retired from the National Research Council.

Backgrounder

Hugh's Inventions

Hugh designed twenty-two electronic instruments. They include:

- Free Reed Organ (1937)
- Electronic Sackbut (1945–48), plus later models
- Touch-Sensitive Organ (1953–57)
- Multi-Track Tape Recorder (1955–64)
- Two-Channel Alternator (1964)
- Polyphone (1970)

1934–

Julia Levy

> " I knew I was going to make research my life. "

Key Events

1955 Graduates with a B.A. degree from the University of British Columbia

1958 Gains a Ph.D. from the University of London, England, and begins teaching at the University of British Columbia

1969 Marries Edwin Levy

1972 Is promoted to professor of microbiology, University of British Columbia

1980 Is elected a fellow of the Royal Society of Canada

1981 Co-founds QLT PhotoTherapeutics Inc.

1982 Is awarded B.C. Science Council Gold Medal for Medical Research

1986 Wins Killam Senior Research Prize

1987 Is appointed to the National Advisory Board of Science and Technology

1995 Becomes president of QLT PhotoTherapeutics

1998 Wins Canadian Woman Entrepreneur of the Year Award

Early Years

Julia was six years old when she left home. It was the beginning of World War II, and Japanese troops were attacking Southeast Asia. Julia's father feared that the Japanese might also attack Indonesia, where Julia and her family lived, and harm his wife and daughters. He sent his family to Canada, where they settled in Vancouver.

After the war, when Julia next saw her father, she hardly recognized him. He was so thin he weighed almost as little as she did. He had spent the war years in a Japanese-run prison camp in very harsh conditions. He never fully recovered. "Don't upset your father," Julia's mother used to say. Julia always had to be careful not to worry her father.

Julia's mother was the strong person in the family. She went to work to support the others. To make it easier for her to work, Julia and her sister attended boarding school for several years.

Shortly before the Japanese army arrived in Indonesia, Julia's father sent Julia (right), her older sister, and their mother to the safety of Canada.

Backgrounder

From Southeast Asia to Canada

Julia was born in Singapore, where her father had a job with a Dutch trading bank. Her father, Guillaume Coppens, was Dutch. Her mother, Dorothy, was English. The family later moved to Indonesia, which was a Dutch colony at the time.

The climate in both Singapore and Indonesia is very hot. When Julia's mother set off for cold Canada in 1940, she made warm woolen dresses for her two daughters. The girls were wearing these thick dresses when they arrived in Canada—in an August heat wave.

Developing Skills

In 1952, Julia enrolled at the University of British Columbia. She wanted to be like her mother and earn a university degree. She had seen how life can suddenly change for the worse, and she knew that her mother's education had helped her get a good job.

Julia was interested in medicine and thought she might become a doctor. At university, she changed her mind. She became fascinated by biochemistry—the chemistry of living things. After gaining her bachelor's degree, she worked for a higher degree in biochemistry. She did this work in England—she had married and her husband wanted to study in England. In 1958, Julia gained a Ph.D. in biochemistry from the University of London.

On returning to Vancouver, Julia taught microbiology at the University of British Columbia. Microbiology is the study of tiny micro-organisms, such as bacteria and viruses. As well as teaching, Julia led a research program. But her marriage was not going as well as her career. By the mid-1960s, she and her husband had parted. She was a single mother supporting two children.

In 1969, Julia married her second husband—Edwin Levy, a fellow scientist. At the time, she was an associate professor at the university. Three years later, she was promoted to full professor. By then, she was deeply involved in research on the immune system.

In 1955, Julia graduated with a bachelor's degree from the University of British Columbia.

The immune system is the collection of molecules and cells that help the body fight disease. Julia was researching ways of increasing the immune system's ability to fight cancer. Her work was going well, and she needed to make an arrangement with a **pharmaceutical company**. The company would then be able to manufacture and sell any medical drugs Julia's team invented. This way, the drugs would be widely available to patients.

Here, Julia ran into a problem. The university could not put her in touch with a pharmaceutical company. Indeed, she could not even find a suitable Canadian company.

She discussed the problem with a colleague, and they decided to form their own company. They called it Quadra Logic Technologies (QLT), which was later changed to QLT PhotoTherapeutics Inc.

> "You have to be able to support yourself. If you can't, the world can suddenly change and you can be left without anything."

As a professor at UBC, Julia's research gave her important clues about how the human body fights cancer.

Backgrounder

QLT

This company, which is based in Vancouver, is now called QLT PhotoTherapeutics. It was formed in 1981 by Julia and four others: John Brown, Jim Miller, Ron McKenzie, and Tony Phillips. Each of them put up $50,000 to get the company started. Julia and her husband Ed had to mortgage their house to raise Julia's share of the money. Ed later joined the company. In 1999, QLT was ranked as one of the fifteen leading biotechnology companies in North America.

Accomplishments

Julia's research took off in an exciting new way because of her children. When they played outdoors at the family's vacation home, they sometimes got blisters on their skin. Julia suspected the blisters were caused by a plant—much the way poison ivy can affect the skin. The odd thing was that the blisters did not always occur, even though the children played in the same area.

Julia discussed the mystery with a scientist friend who specialized in plants. He asked her if the children could have brushed against cow parsley—a plant with white flowers. Yes, Julia said. Her friend explained that cow parsley contains substances that are **photosensitive**. It harms the skin only when the skin is exposed to sunlight. That was why the children's skin blistered only some of the time.

Julia's friend told her that an American pharmaceutical company had made a drug called Photofrin. Like cow parsley, Photofrin became active only when exposed to light. There was hope that it could be used to treat diseases. Tests were being done to see how well it worked against cancer.

This was exciting news, and Julia started a research project on photosensitive drugs. She and a research associate made a photosensitive drug called Verteporfin. They then started testing it. Before a drug can be put on the market, it must be tested very thoroughly, first on animals and then on a group of patients who agree to take part in the research. The tests on patients are known as "clinical trials."

Julia was awarded a National Merit Award in 1999 by the Ottawa Life Science Council.

While Verteporfin was being developed, Julia heard that the company that owned Photofrin could not afford to continue its clinical trials. QLT and another company bought the rights to Photofrin so that they could carry on the trials. They found that Photofrin worked well as a treatment for several types of cancer, including cancer of the lung, esophagus, and bladder. In the mid-1990s, it was given government approval for cancer treatment.

Verteporfin looks even more promising than Photofrin. As well as being effective against cancer, it may become a new form of treatment for a wide range of diseases. The clinical trials of Verteporfin have gone so well that QLT has become a very successful company. Julia was made president of the company in 1995, and in 1998 she received the Canadian Woman Entrepreneur of the Year Award.

> **Go for it! Women can do anything.**

Julia has drawn love and support from her second husband, Edwin, and their dog Lucy.

Backgrounder

How Photosensitive Drugs Work Against Cancer

The drug is injected into the bloodstream of the person suffering from cancer. The blood carries the drug through the person's body. Surgeons then shine a laser light on the area where the cancer has grown. The light destroys the cancer cells. It is a combination of the drug plus the light that has this effect. Cells in the rest of the body are not harmed by the drug because they are not exposed to light.

The advantage of photosensitive treatment is that it allows a surgeon to target the diseased area and leave the rest of the body unaffected. Previously, drugs that worked against cancer weakened the entire body.

1861–1939

James Naismith

> 66 I decided that the only real satisfaction that I would ever derive from life was to help my fellow beings. 99

Key Events

1887   Earns a bachelor's degree from McGill University, Montreal

1890   Graduates from Presbyterian College, Montreal, and is licensed to be a Presbyterian minister

1890   Goes to YMCA training school at Springfield, Massachusetts

1891   Invents basketball

1898   Earns the degree of doctor of medicine from Gross Medical College, Denver, Colorado

1898   Is appointed athletics coach, director of physical education, and religious director at the University of Kansas

1917   Is sent to France as a representative of YMCA during World War I

1936   Is honoured as the Father of Basketball at the Olympic Games in Berlin

Early Years

Jim stood at the edge of the frozen pond watching his friends skate. He wished he had a pair of skates, but he did not want to ask his uncle. Uncle Peter expected Jim to solve his own problems.

Grandpa had been like that, too. "Don't think you can't do it," he would say whenever Jim faced something difficult. "Go on! Give it a try!" His grandfather had died three years before. His mother and father had died the same year. Uncle Peter now acted as father to Jim and his brother and sister. They lived on the family farm near Almonte, Ontario.

Jim often helped out on the farm, and he knew how to use the tools in the workshop. He decided to make his own skates. He made the blades by sharpening two steel files. He then fixed the files into strips of wood, which he strapped to his boots. At twelve years old, Jim was already being inventive.

> " Baseball is good,... soccer is an excellent game,... lacrosse is an ideal game,... and basket-ball is for the winter months, indoors, what the above games are for outdoors. "

In elementary school, James was a natural athlete and a leader in many physical activities.

Backgrounder

Hockey

When Jim and his friends gathered on the pond in winter, they did not play hockey. The game had not yet been invented. Hockey, as we know it today, was first played in Montreal in 1875. It was made up by some McGill students. The first organized team was the McGill University Hockey Club, which was formed in 1879.

Developing Skills

Jim was usually the leader of his group of friends. He was good at sports and clever at thinking up things to do. But he was not good at schoolwork. Jim dropped out of school when he was fifteen. For the next five years, he worked in logging camps each winter and on the farm each summer.

After a few years, Jim realized he had made a mistake. He wished he had stayed in school. The principal of Almonte high school agreed to take him back, even though Jim was twenty years old. Jim was twenty-two when he gained his high school diploma.

Jim needed the diploma because he wanted to go to university. He wanted to become a minister. Jim's family belonged to the Presbyterian church, and he had been brought up to be very religious. Being a Presbyterian minister seemed a good way of helping other people.

In 1883, Jim enrolled at McGill University. There he soon made his name as an athlete. He was especially good at gymnastics and rugby football. Jim continued to play rugby after he graduated from McGill and began training as a minister. To pay for his studies at Presbyterian College, he took a job teaching physical education.

Although he is known for inventing basketball, James (third row from the top, left) was a rugby star during his years at McGill University.

Before long, Jim's studies were taking second place to gymnastics and rugby. The principal of Presbyterian College advised Jim to give up sports—or drop the idea of becoming a minister. Jim was having doubts, too. One day on the rugby field, the player next to him let out a string of swear words, but he stopped when he realized who was listening. "I beg your pardon, Jim," he said. "I forgot you were there."

These words changed Jim's life. His aim was still the same—to be a good influence on people. But he thought he could do it better by working among them as a sports instructor, rather than preaching to them from a pulpit. Therefore, when Jim completed the course at the college, he did not become a minister. He took up physical education full time.

> 66 *There must be some natural attraction in sports that could be used to lead young men to a good end.* 99

As a Phys Ed teacher at the University of Kansas, James taught a variety of different sports, including fencing.

Backgrounder

Jim's Football Helmet

When Jim played football, nobody ever wore a helmet. To protect his ears, Jim flattened them with adhesive tape. That did not work very well, so he tried wrapping a strip of cloth around his head. Finally, he hit on the idea of wearing a football cut in half. It was an early type of helmet, possibly the first ever worn.

Accomplishments

>>>>>>

QUICK NOTES

▶ When Jim was in his thirties, he studied medicine. He felt that a physical education instructor should be able to treat injuries.

▶ Although Jim was the inventor of basketball, he played the game only twice in his life.

▶ On the farm near Almonte, where Jim grew up, one can visit the Dr. James Naismith Centre.

▶ The Naismith Basketball Hall of Fame is in Springfield, Massachusetts.

Jim became an instructor at the YMCA training school in Springfield, Massachusetts. This was the perfect place for him, because it was a Christian college and stressed athletics. The aim was to produce healthy young people with good characters. Although a range of subjects were taught, Bible study and sport were the most important.

In 1891, the principal asked Jim to think up an indoor game that the students could play between the football and baseball seasons. Jim tried out versions of football and other games, but they caused too many injuries when played indoors. Running with the ball must not be allowed, he decided. Tackling must be forbidden, too. As for the goal, it must be something small—a box or basket. But it must be above ground level. Otherwise the defenders could simply sit in it to prevent a goal being scored.

There was a high spectators' balcony surrounding the Springfield gymnasium, and Jim asked the janitor to fix a box at each end. The janitor did not have any boxes. "But I have two peach baskets," he said. That is how basketball began. The bottom was left in the baskets, so the ball had to be picked out each time a player scored.

The first suggestion for the name of the new game was "Naismith ball" but James did not like this suggestion. The name "basketball" was suggested by a student in one of his classes.

> 66 *If the player can't run with the ball, we don't have to tackle. And if we don't have to tackle, the roughness is eliminated.* 99

The first game was played in December 1891, and before long, many people were playing basketball. It became popular quickly because it was fun to play and needed little equipment—just a ball, two baskets, and a ladder to pick the ball out of the basket. Open basketball nets were not introduced until 1906. By then, the game was being played in many countries throughout the world.

As Jim grew older, he became famous as a promoter of physical fitness. For many years, he taught and coached at the University of Kansas. His moment of glory came in 1936, when basketball was first played at the Olympic Games. Jim was present at the Olympic ceremonies in Berlin and had the honour of tossing up the first ball in the first game. Later that year, Jim was elected president of the International Federation of Basketball Leagues.

James married Maude Sherman in 1894. Together they had five children.

Backgrounder

A Strong Body and Clean Mind

During World War I, Jim was sent overseas to talk to the troops and listen to their problems. He gave them the same advice he always gave his students—to be healthy and clean-living. That was the way Jim himself tried to live. On the inside of his Bible, he had written:

> I will be a man
> Strong in body
> Clean in mind
> Lofty in ideals

MORE GREAT CANADIANS

Here are a few more Canadian inventors. The Suggested Reading list will help you find others. *Horizon Canada* is a good source to try. It is an eleven-volume collection of more than a hundred magazines. Each of the magazines features a Canadian inventor or discoverer on the inside back cover.

1929–

Nestor Burtnyk

Creator of Computer Animation Programs

Nestor became interested in computer **graphics** in the late 1960s. He had the idea of applying computer graphics to the movie industry. In those days, thousands of drawings were needed to create a cartoon film like those by Walt Disney. First, the chief "animator" drew a type of comic strip telling the story. Then other artists drew all the connecting pictures.

Nestor invented a way by which a computer could draw all the connecting pictures. The National Film Board of Canada and Hollywood studios were soon using Nestor's computer programs. Nestor and his associate researcher, Marceli Wein, won an Academy Award for the invention.

1961–

Tim Collings

Inventor of the V-Chip

The V-Chip is a gadget that can be used in the home to block television programs. Parents can use the V-Chip to prevent their children from watching unsuitable programs. Tim first had the idea of making a program blocker in 1989. He later set up a company to sell his invention. Tim is involved in numerous other research projects.

Nestor Burtnyk

1838–1893

Georges-Edouard Desbarats

Inventor of Halftone Photographic Printing

The halftone process made it possible to print photographs. Georges and his engraver friend William Leggo invented the process in the 1860s. Before then, publishers had to use line drawings or engravings if they wanted to include pictures in publications.

In the halftone process, a photo is photographed through a screen. This turns the picture into tiny dots of various sizes. The world's first photos printed by this method appeared in Georges' magazine, *Canadian Illustrated News*, in 1869. Halftone printing is still used today.

1929–

Graeme Ferguson

Filmmaker and co-founder of Imax Corporation

Imax's technology was shown in 1970 at the world's fair in Osaka, Japan. This giant-screen presentation was the brainchild of Graeme and two fellow Canadian filmmakers, Robert Kerr and Roman Kroitor. They recruited William Shaw, a Toronto engineer, to build a special projector for Imax. The following year, the first IMAX® theatre opened at Ontario Place in Toronto. In 1973, the company also began to make IMAX® Dome films, which are projected onto a huge domed screen, whereas IMAX® technology uses a flat surface. There are now special IMAX® theatres throughout the world showing their unique large-format films.

Graeme Ferguson

1866–1932

Reginald Fessenden

Radio Inventor

Reginald found a way of sending speech and music long distances without using telephone wires. In 1900, he transmitted the first words ever sent by radio. They were received by his assistant, Alfred Thiessen, who was a kilometre away. Then, in 1906, Reginald made the world's first public radio broadcast. It included the sound of Reginald playing the violin. The message was received by some ships at sea. Some of Reginald's inventions were used, without his consent, during World War I. He was later recognized for these designs.

1827–1915

Sir Sandford Fleming

Inventor of Standard Time

Sandford was a great engineer and railway builder. When working on long-distance railways across Canada, he found it very awkward that different cities set their clocks at different times. Other countries had the same problem, too.

Sandford worked out a system that divided the world into twenty-four time zones. All clocks within each zone would keep the same time. In 1884, Sandford's system of Standard Time was adopted by a number of countries at an international conference. Other countries soon followed. Today, all countries use Sandford's system.

1915–

James Hillier

Electron Microscope Inventor

James built one of the world's first electron microscopes. This was in the 1930s, when James was a graduate student at the University of Toronto. A fellow student, Albert Prebus, worked with him on the project, which had been suggested by the physics professor, Eli Burton. An electron microscope is far more powerful than an ordinary microscope. It can make things appear 30,000 times larger than they are. James' first microscope magnified objects 7,000 times.

James continued his research at RCA Laboratories and Melpar Inc. By the time he retired in 1977, James was the executive vice-president and senior scientist at RCA. During his career, James received forty-one patents for his inventions.

1915–1998

Harold Johns

Designed the Cobalt-60 "Bomb"

In the early 1950s, when he was a professor at the University of Saskatchewan, Harold designed a machine called the cobalt-60 bomb. Before this invention, radiation treatment was only available if the cancer was close to the surface. The new machine gave off rays strong enough to destroy cancer cells deep inside the body. It led to great advances in the treatment of cancer and new hope for people suffering from the disease. Harold was made an Officer of the Order of Canada, and in 1983 he received the Medal of Honour from the Canadian Medical Association.

1946–

Audrey McQuarrie

Wheatheat Inventor

Audrey calls her invention "Wheatheat" because it uses both wheat and heat (though it can also be used as a cold pack). Wheatheat packs are little cushions filled with grain. When heated (or frozen) and placed on a part of the body that is aching, they can ease the pain. They are used for such ailments as headaches and muscle strain. Audrey had the help of the Inventor's Assistance Program at the University of Waterloo when looking for a way to promote her invention.

Audrey McQuarrie

1914–

Bruce Nodwell

Inventor of Tracked Vehicles

The first successful tracked vehicles for use on muskeg were invented by Bruce Nodwell of Calgary in the early 1950s. Tracked vehicles grip the ground with beltlike **tracks** instead of tires. This allows them to move across marshy or sandy ground without sinking in. The Nodwell Tracked Truck was especially useful to the oil industry in Canada's North, transporting heavy drilling equipment over waterlogged ground. By the mid-1950s, Bruce's machines earned the reputation for being the best vehicles for tough western Canadian terrain.

Bruce has designed many other vehicles for use in difficult areas. These include the buses which today carry tourists across the Columbia Icefield.

1867–1937

Sir Charles Saunders

Developer of Marquis Wheat

In 1904, Charles developed the first few heads of Marquis wheat. He bred them from Red Fife, a wheat strain that was also developed by a Canadian—David Fife of Ontario. Although Red Fife was very popular in eastern Canada, it did not ripen quickly enough to be suitable for the prairies. All too often, the crop was killed by frost before it could be harvested. Once Marquis wheat became available, the prairie wheat crop more than doubled. Canada became famous throughout the world for its huge crops of high-quality wheat.

Rachel Zimmerman

1972–

Rachel Zimmerman

Inventor of the Blissymbol Printer

The Blissymbol Printer is a computer-controlled device that enables people suffering from **cerebral palsy** to write messages. Usually, people with cerebral palsy have difficulty speaking or writing. Rachel's invention gives them a way of communicating with others. At the Canada-Wide Science Fair in 1985, at the age of twelve, Rachel won the silver medal for her invention. The following year, she represented Canada at the World Exhibition of Achievements of Young Inventors, held in Bulgaria. Rachel is hoping to improve her invention. She wants to add Hebrew text as well as a modem and voice output to her design. Rachel is currently employed at the Canadian Space Agency in St-Hubert, Quebec.

GLOSSARY

amputated: surgically cut off a limb because of disease or injury

anesthetic: a substance that causes an entire or partial loss of feeling or pain

cerebral palsy: a condition that people are born with, often causing parts of the body to be weak or paralysed

elocution: clear and well-expressed speaking

gangrene: dead tissue in part of the body where blood has been prevented from circulating

graphics: drawings, charts, and other illustrative material

hydrofoil: a boat that skims the top of the water's surface. When it moves quickly, its front end lifts out of the water.

hypothermia: abnormally low body temperature; produced by exposure to cold air or water

patent: a piece of paper provided by the government giving an inventor the sole right to make and sell an invention

pharmaceutical company: a company that makes medical drugs and medicines

photosensitive: being affected by light

physiology: the science dealing with the normal functions of living things or their parts

probe: a slender instrument used in surgery

radar: a device that finds and tracks distant objects by the reflection of radio waves

synthesizer: an electronic machine that can create and change the sounds of musical instruments

tracks: continuous bands around the wheels of vehicles such as tanks and some trucks and tractors

transmitter: the part of the telephone that sends out the message

tuberculosis: an infectious disease that can affect any tissue of the body, especially the lungs

turbine: an engine or motor driven by a current of air, water, or steam that pushes against the blades of a wheel; the wheels and drive shaft turn, creating energy

SUGGESTED READING

Black, Harry. *Canadian Scientists and Inventors: Biographies of People Who Made a Difference.* Markham: Pembroke, 1997.

Brown, J.J. *The Inventors: Great Ideas in Canadian Enterprise.* Toronto: McClelland and Stewart, 1967.

Horizon Canada: The New Way to Discover Canada. 11 volumes. Brampton: Centre for the Study and Teaching of Canada, 1987.

MacLeod, Elizabeth. *Alexander Graham Bell: An Inventive Life.* Toronto: Kids Can Press, 1999.

Mayer, Roy. *Inventing Canada: One Hundred Years of Innovation.* Vancouver: Raincoast Books, 1997.

Wallace, Elizabeth. *The Book for Women Who Invent or Want To.* Waterloo: Women Inventors Project, 1989.

Webb, Michael. *Armand Bombardier: Inventor of the Snowmobile.* Mississauga: Copp Clark Pitman, 1991.

INDEX

Baldwin, F.W. "Casey" 10

basketball 4, 36, 37, 38, 40, 41

Bell, Alexander Melville 7

biochemistry 32

Blissymbol Printer 45

Brown, John 33

Callaghan, John 15

cobalt-60 "bomb" 44

computer animation 42

electron microscope 44

Electronic Sackbut 24, 28, 29

Free Reed Organ 29

halftone photographic printing 42

heart pacemaker 12, 16

hockey 4, 37

Hopps, John 15, 16

hydrofoil 6, 10, 46

hypothermia 12, 14, 15, 16, 17, 46

IMAX 4, 43

Levy, Edwin 30, 32

Marquis wheat 45

McCurdy, J.A. Douglas 11

McKenzie, Ron 33

microbiology 30, 32

Miller, Jim 33

Morse, Samuel 9

Multi-Track Tape Recorder 24, 29

National Film Board of Canada 42

National Research Council of Canada 15, 24, 26, 27, 28, 29

patent 5, 18, 21, 22, 46

photosensitive drugs 34, 35, 46

Polyphone 24, 29

QLT PhotoTherapeutics 30, 33, 35

radar 26, 46

radio broadcasting 4, 43

Robb, Frank Morse 27

Sea-Doo 23

Ski-Doo 18, 22, 23

snowmobile 4, 18, 19, 20, 21, 22, 23

Standard Time 43

telegraph 8, 9

telephone 4, 6, 10, 43, 46

Touch-Sensitive Organ 24, 29

tracked vehicles 45

Two-Channel Alternator 29

V-Chip 42

Visible Speech 7, 8

Watson, Thomas 9, 10

wheatheat 44

World War I 36, 41, 43

World War II 14, 22, 26, 31